PROPERTY OF:

INSIGHTS
an imprint of
INSIGHT EDITIONS
www.insighteditions.com

Manufactured in China
10 9 8 7 6 5 4 3 2 1